Deploy!

Rapid Deployment Guide for Web Applications

James Gibson
and
Steve Spalding

Copyright © 2013
Innovate GSB LLC
All rights reserved.
ISBN - 978-1-304-01799-4

Part 0
Introduction

This guide is designed to help you take your idea and turn it into a functioning web application. It isn't the be-all and the end-all of launching a web app; rather, it provides a starting point that will let you take your application live with a minimum of errors.

This is not a programming tutorial, though it will suggest some resources to help with that. It also won't tell you how to set up your application to handle a hundred million users, or even a hundred thousand users. Our goal is to get your application deployed- if success becomes a problem, that bridge can be crossed when it matters.

What this guide will help you do is deploy applications based on WordPress and PHP, the web's most popular content management system and scripting language respectively; it will also help you create applications based on Ruby on Rails, a popular dynamic web framework used by many famous services including Twitter. Ruby on Rails is based on Ruby, another popular scripting language.

We have also included a short section on setting up Wordpress on a simple VPS, which may be enough for you if your project doesn't require a lot of custom code and won't experience too much load. The true purpose of this document, however, is to show you how to configure a server from the bottom up, completely from scratch, using Amazon Web Service's cloud.

It is worth noting that there are a lot of ways to do this, and the way that we are outlining isn't the "easiest". This guide shows you how to deploy a development environment and server from the ground up, top to bottom. If pure ease is what you are looking for, a better choice might be a managed services like EngineYard or Heroku. They can save a lot of time and effort, since you do not have to worry about installing software or configuring anything.

However, it is worth learning how to do things from scratch. First, managed services cost money. The same amount of processing power from EngineYard or Heroku can cost twice or three times as much as renting directly from Amazon. If your application is sufficiently large or profitable, this can be a great trade off - at some point, your time is worth more than that small amount of money, but if you're just starting out that is probably not the case. Second, even if you end up using a managed service, it is worth understanding the full stack, from soup to nuts. Understanding how the different parts fit together will help you make better business decisions and write better code.

This guide does assume a certain level of familiarity with technology; however, a clever reader can easily follow by googling any term they don't understand and reading the relevant Wikipedia article. In fact, this brings us to the zeroth rule of development:

The 0th Rule

When you're learning how to program or how to develop an application, you'll run into problems. Frequently. Things break, errors get thrown, programs behave unexpectedly. This happens, and should be expected.

The 0th rule acknowledges this, and provides a solution: google it. If an error message is spit out, paste it into the search bar (or a few key terms). If you can't get something set up, google what you're trying to do, and what platform you're on. Add the search term "tutorial" if you're just starting on something - someone has probably put together a guide for you.

Click on a link, and if it doesn't give you what you need, click on another. One of them will almost certainly have a solution for you - but the only way to find out if what is posted will solve your problem is to try doing what the guides and help files you end up finding suggest. So, if it tells you to run a command, actually do it. Chances are, at least at first, it won't help, but if you do this enough, you'll be surprised how quickly you become a knowledgeable developer - or at least able to pretend to be one.

What?

If this is your first foray into web programming, you might not be familiar with some of the terms that will be thrown around. In addition, having a mental model of how the half-dozen moving parts that we will be assembling fit together will make things easier to understand. So let's begin our journey there.

What constitutes a web application? To be a *web* application, a program has to be delivered via the web, into a web **browser** like Microsoft's Internet Explorer, Mozilla's Firefox, or Google Chrome. You are familiar with a web browser, in fact, it is probably your most used application.

A browser is responsible for retrieving and displaying content from a **server**. "Server" is a general term that describes a computer's role in a system. In a client-server model, the server stores all the information for a program, and is responsible for executing it. The results are sent to a client which can then issue commands to the server.

For example, Google's search engine uses a client-server model; you send a search request to Google using your client (a web browser), Google's servers execute a program to perform the search, and the results are sent back to the client to be displayed. On the other hand, Microsoft Word (before Office 365) is not a client-server model; the Word program is stored on your computer and all of the processing takes place there.

Your web application runs on your server. The server has to run several pieces of software: first, of course, an operating system. Then, a **web server**, which is in charge of processing requests from clients and sending information back to them. The web server passes its dynamic content to a **script processor** which executes the code for your web application. Your program will need to store and access data, which is stored in a **database.** Note that "web server" can refer to either just the web server component, or the entire machine, complete with web server, script processor, and database.

Although chances are you run Windows as your operating system (and we'll show you how to set up your development environment on Windows), our servers will be using the open-source and free

Linux operating system. Linux is the most popular choice for web servers and is fast, secure, and free.

In fact, we will only use free and open source software to deploy. We'll be using nginx (pronounced "engine-x") as our web server. Other web servers include Apache (the most common) and Lighttpd. For our script processor, we will show you how to use PHP or Ruby on Rails - other possible choices include Python, Perl, or Java Server Pages. For your database, we'll show you how to setup and use both MySQL, Oracle's popular and free relational database system, or MongoDB, an interesting and new nonrelational database.

In addition, we'll provide some tips and resources for getting your development started, including templates, themes, code libraries, and other resources you can use to speed development. Making use of preexisting resources allows you to deploy faster and focus on your value add, instead of wasting effort recreating the wheel.

There are a few other terms you'll need to be familiar with. You are certainly familiar with **urls**, which are the alphanumeric addresses for internet resources, like http://google.com, or http://projectmona.com/the-manifesto/. These strings of letters identify specific resources on the web. The core part of a url is the **domain name** - in Google's case, google.com, or in ProjectMONA's case, projectmona.com. The domain name includes the top-level domain (.com, .net, .org, .co.uk, etc) and the second-level domain (projectmona, google, etc). If you want to host a website, you'll need a domain name, which can be purchased from a **registrar** like NameCheap or GoDaddy.

However, the domain name is just a human-readable address. A web browser can only send requests to an **ip address** ("internet protocol" address). IP addresses are either groups of numbers between 0 and 255 (like 54.235.135.78, an IPv4 address) or, in the new IPv6 standard, 8 groups of 16 bits (for example, 2001:0db8:0000:0000:0000:ff00:0042:8329). We will be using IPv4, so be familiar with the x.x.x.x format.

Every device on the internet has an IP address, including the web server we'll be setting up. Special servers called **dns servers** ("domain name system servers") translate domain names to IP addresses. So, if ProjectMONA.com is hosted on a server with ip address 54.235.135.78 (at time of writing, it is), then there is a DNS server which will tell your web browser that if the browser wants to request a page from projectmona.com, it should direct its request to 54.235.135.78.

The DNS system is quite complex - if you want to learn more about it, there is plenty of information on the internet. For now, just know that you need a DNS server to let people access your website, since it translates domain names into ip addresses. Most hosting providers have a DNS service included in the hosting cost, if not, there are other services that can be used.
At this point, we've described a lot of moving parts, so let's recap the whole process of how a request gets served by your web application.

A user opens their web browser and enters the url (which has the domain name you registered as a part of it) for some page on your web application. Their web browser sends a request to a DNS server (which you set up using your hosting provider's service), and receives the ip address for your server. The web browser then sends a request to your server for the page.

This request is picked up by your web server program (nginx). The web server process the request, and figures out which part of the program to run, passing that information to the script processor. The script processor runs a program that you wrote or set up (for example, WordPress), and may access the database in order to do so. The script processor then generates some results, passes these to the web server, which then sends them out back to the user's web browser, which displays them on the page.

This whole process, in a best case scenario, takes well under a second. Depending on the query - for example, if the program that is being processed takes a long time to execute - it could take longer.

But I don't know how to program!

This may not be as big of a problem as you think. Depending on how complex your idea is, you may be able to build it by simply assembling pre-existing pieces of code- you will be amazed at what you can do with the right combination of WordPress plugins. Chances are you will have to learn how to code, though, but this is a lot easier than you think.

Unfortunately, this document will not help you with that. Instead we suggest that you first read the section on setting up a development environment, then go read a couple "how to program" to tutorials. In particular, The Pragmatic Programmer publishes several very good programming books, including an excellent book on Rails. Perhaps better for the true beginner, Tizag.com has a truly fantastic series on learning PHP and MySQL.

Some advice on learning your first programming language: first, programming isn't a spectator sport. Just reading other people's code isn't enough to truly understand how the machine works; you must tinker with it, break it, and put it back together.

Second, it is useful to keep *A Programmer's Lament* in mind:

I really hate this damned machine
I wish that they would sell it.
It never does quite what I want
But only what I tell it.

(Taken from Joseph Gallian's *Contemporary Abstract Algebra*, originally from Dennie Van Tassel's *The Compleat Computer*).

The core insight of the lament is that the challenge of computer programming isn't figuring out what you want the computer to do, it is accurately and rigorously translating what you want the computer to do into specific instructions that the computer can understand. When things don't work as you think they should, it is usually not because the computer is doing something wrong, but rather that it is doing exactly what you told it to do. What you told it to do, however, may not be what you wanted it to do at all.

Part 1
The Development Environment

Before we can *deploy* an application to the internet, we need an application. To build one, we need to be able to run one, so that we can test it and see what it will look like before it goes live. To accomplish this what we really need is a **development environment**, a copy of the software, stored your own computer, used to see how the final production product will look and feel.

For web programming, half of the problem is already solved. In your development environment, you'll access the web application in the same way you'd access a real, live application - through your web browser. You already have one installed - probably either Internet Explorer, Firefox, or Chrome. If you only have one, it's a good idea to install one or both of the others, since sometimes your website can look different in different browsers.

Remember that we're assuming you're running Windows for the purposes of this guide. We'll include some tips for Mac OSX and Linux users in the appendix.

Setting up PHP and MySQL for Wordpress

WordPress is written in PHP, a popular scripting (programming) language. It uses MySQL, a popular and free database engine, to store data. Since a Linux server with an Apache webserver, MySQL, and PHP is the most common web server configuration in existence, there is a special term for it - the LAMP (**L**inux, **A**pache, **M**ySQL, **P**HP) stack. If you use Windows instead of Linux, it's called the WAMP stack.

Luckily, there is a great free software package called XAMPP (pronounced either "zamp" or "x amp") that provides a single-step installation of everything you need. To install it, go to http://www.apachefriends.org/en/xampp.html

and find the link for "XAMPP for Windows". You'll want to click that link and scroll down the resulting page until you find a "Download" section. There should be a subsection called "XAMPP Windows 1.8.1" (at the time of writing, there may be a new version with a different version number). Find the link under that section that says "Installer". It should take you to a page on SourceForge and automatically begin downloading the program - if your browser asks you if you want to download the file which "may harm your computer", tell it to keep the file or allow the download.

When the installer is finished downloading, open it like you would any program.

When given the option, you do not need to check any of the boxes for installing Apache, MySQL, or FileZilla as a service. Then click "Install" - the installer will take care of the rest.

When you're done, you can go ahead and start the XAMPP control panel by clicking on the icon on your desktop or selecting XAMPP from the start menu. The control panel has buttons labeled "Start" for Apache, MySQL, and FileZilla. Click "Start" for each of these. If FileZilla says that it must be installed as a service, check the "Svc" box on the far left next to FileZilla, accept all the prompts, and then start the service. If Windows raises security warnings, allow access for everything.

When each of the categories included indicates "Running...", you're ready to go. Open your web browser and enter "localhost" in the address bar. If everything went according to plan, you should see a nice "XAMPP" splash screen. Click "English" on the bottom bar, and behold the control panel.

From here, you can view the status of your development server and all sorts of other fun stuff. The XAMPP control panel runs on PHP, so we have everything we need to install WordPress setup.

Setting up Wordpress

First, though, we need an FTP client. (see our "Easy Mode" section for instructions on installing WinSCP)

Once you have WinSCP set up, we're ready to install WordPress. Download WordPress from http://wordpress.org/ by following the download link. You should end up with a wordpress-some-version-number.zip file. Extract the files to a place you will recognize by right clicking and hitting "Extract".

Then, upload these files to the server using WinSCP. Connect to the server with hostname "localhost" using the protocol "FTP" and username "newuser". The password is "wampp". When you've logged in, copy the entire "wordpress" directory that you extracted to the server.

When the files are finished copying (it may take a minute), you should be able to open your web browser and enter the url http://localhost/wordpress. You should see a page telling you that there is no wp-config.php file, and asking if you want to create it. You do, so click "Create Configuration File".

Assuming there were no errors, you should be presented with a page topped by the "WordPress" logo, telling you that you will need a few items to proceed, including your database name and credentials. We don't have that yet, so set this page aside and open a new tab. Send the new tab to http://localhost, and find the link to "PHPMyAdmin" on the bottom of the left-hand navigation bar.

Setting up the Database

PHPMyAdmin is a web-based tool for administering MySQL databases. It allows you to view the databases, tables, and records that are stored on your server. We're going to create a new MySQL database - a database being a logical container for all data that belongs to a single application. One server can host multiple databases.

In PHPMyAdmin, click the top "Databases" tab. Near the bottom of the screen, there should be a field for "Create a New Database". Enter the name "wordpress" (or, some other name that makes sense - you can leave the "Collation" drop down field as "Collation". After clicking "Create", you should be taken to the database management screen. The left bar should now include a database "wordpress" (or the name you entered) at the bottom.

You can use PHPMyAdmin to create tables, enter data, and view data manually, but it's more fun and more efficient to let

WordPress do the work. Switch back to the wordpress tab we opened before, which tells you which pieces of information you need and has the "Let's Go!" button at the bottom. Click "Let's Go!".

You should be presented with a form which will allow you to enter your Database Name, [database] User Name, [database] Password, Database Host, and Table Prefix. The Database name should be pre-populated with "wordpress" - if you entered "wordpress" in the "Create a Database" field earlier, leave that as is; if not, change it to whatever you entered as the database name. For user name, use "root", and make the password field blank. The host should remain "localhost" (that's the domain name of the computer you're on), and the table prefix can stay as "wp_". When you've completed the form, click the submit button.

If everything works, you should be greeted with a friendly "All right, sparky!" message and the option to continue the install. Do so.

At this point, you will be presented with a screen to set a few parameters for your new WordPress site. Set the site title, admin username, a password, and your email address. Go ahead and uncheck the "allow search engines to index this site" - for a development environment, we don't need that.

Since this installation of WordPress is only on your local machine and is only accessible for development, you don't need to worry about your password strength. When you deploy WordPress to a live website later, though, you absolutely should guarantee you have a full-strength password.

Once you hit "Install", WordPress will do a little processing, and you'll end up with a "Success!" message. Your WordPress development environment is now ready to go, and is accessible (when you're running XAMPP) from the url http://localhost/wordpress.

Final Touches

Once you have WordPress installed, there is a lot you can do with it. Check out our "Easy Mode" section for more information on customizing wordpress.

You can also run generic PHP scripts on your new website. Just use WinSCP to upload your .php files to the server in the same way you uploaded the WordPress files. They'll be accessible in your browser at http://localhost/yourfilename.php, or, if you put them in a folder, http://localhost/foldername/yourfilename.php.

Note that to edit the PHP scripts, you'll want to use a programmer's text editor. Notepad++ (available from notepad-plus-plus.org) is a great choice, though you can use Windows' built-in Notepad or other text editors as well. Note that a text editor is *not the same as a word processor*: you don't want to use Microsoft Word or Libre Office to write code, as code can't have any of the formatting information that Word has to include.

Setting up Ruby on Rails

Ruby on Rails is a web framework that allows you to easily build complex programs in the Ruby language. One of the main benefits of Rails is that it comes with ActiveRecord, which is an Object-Relational Mapper. We'll get into this more later - for now, know that it makes your life much easier by hiding the database from your code.

Of course, in order to let Rails hide the database from your code, there has to be a database to hide. Rails is perfectly at home using one of a large set of databases, including SQLite, NoSQL databases like MongoDB, or the same MySQL that we installed before. To make life easier, we're going to use MySQL, which you can install using the same XAMPP package we discussed in the previous section.

So, if you haven't, go install XAMPP now. However, instead of starting Apache, MySQL, and FileZilla, you only need to start MySQL and Apache. However, don't bother uploading any WordPress files, and instead of creating a database called "wordpress", create a database called "rails" - or any other name that makes sense.

Time to download Ruby on Rails. Point your browser at http://rubyonrails.org/download and find the link for "Windows Installer" under the "Ruby:" heading. Go ahead and download the AMD-64 ".exe" for the newest version of Ruby available - the url should be something along the lines of rubyinstaller-2.0.0-p0-x64.exe, though likely with different numbers for the 2.0.0 and p0.

> **Technical Note:** We specified the "AMD-64" version because most computers today are 64-bit. (Technical fun

fact: 64-bit refers to the number of bits in the memory address space of your processor). If you have an older computer (before about 2007) you probably have a 32 bit processor, so you should download the "rubyinstaller-2.0.0-p0.exe" version, without the "x64". If you aren't sure, try downloading the 64 bit version, and if it doesn't run, download the 32 bit version instead.

When the .exe file is finished downloading (and you've dismissed any security warnings that Windows provides), open it. Go ahead and accept English as the language (unless you're a native speaker of some other language) and accept the license agreement. Go ahead and check the "Add Ruby Extensions to your PATH" and "Associate .rb and .rbw files with this Ruby installation" boxes, and accept the default installation path. After you click "Install", the installer will run, and you should soon be greeted with a "Finished!" screen.

RubyGems

You now have Ruby installed, but now we need to put it on Rails. To do so, we're going to install RubyGems, a package manager for ruby. "Gems" are bits of code, a lot like code libraries, that you can easily import into your application. Most of them are free to use and allow you to save a lot of effort by using other people's code instead of re-inventing the wheel yourself.

Head back to http://rubyonrails.org/download and find the "Download" link under the "Ruby Gems" heading. You'll be taken to the rubgems.org download page. Find the link that says "ZIP" and save the file to a location you will remember. Extract the files in the zip you just downloaded (right click on the folder and select "Extract" or "Extract All"). Open the new folder that was just extracted and find the file that says "setup". Double click it to run it - an old-style "command prompt" or terminal window should appear, with some messages about installing documentation and such. When it disappears, ruby gems is installed.

Now that we have gems installed, we can install the Rails framework with almost no effort at all, since rails is nothing but a ruby gem. Open a command prompt (in Windows 7, hit the Windows button in the bottom-right corner and type "cmd.exe" in the "Search Programs and Files" field, then hit enter). You should be presented with another black terminal window, complete with a flashing cursor waiting for your command.

In the terminal, type

gem install rails

and hit enter. After a few moments (if your internet connection is slow, it may take a few minutes) the terminal will fill with "Fetching" messages. If everything works, you'll end up with another prompt and flashing cursor, a message about "X gems installed" (where X is probably 4) and no "ERROR" messages in the log. If you get messages asking if you want to "overwrite the executable [yN]" go ahead and type "y", then hit enter - this just tells RubyGems to go ahead and install the correct version of a few other programs.

When you're done, you have everything set up and ready to go. The only caveat is that you probably aren't used to using the command prompt. Although there are ways to put a friendly application interface on Rails, we're not going to do so - when you deploy the server, you're going to have to use a linux terminal entirely, so it won't hurt to get used to it.

A Crash Course on the Terminal

If you're already familiar with the terminal, here is the quick version (if not, read skip this short part and read this section): make a new directory, navigate to it, and run

rails new myprojectname

with your project name instead of "myprojectname" (a fine default is "test") which will create a new folder "myprojectname" with the skeleton of a rails application in it.

To start your rails development server, run the command

rails server

in the "myprojectname" directory. You can access the server by pointing your browser at http://localhost:3000. You can move on to the next section.

The terminal you still have open probably has a prompt along the lines of "C:\Users\James>", where "James" is replaced with your user name on your computer. This is the folder that you're currently working out of in the terminal - your user folder is the folder that contains the folders you're more familiar with, like "Documents", "Downloads", "Music", and so on.

You can prove this to yourself by making Windows show you what's in the folder that you are currently in on the terminal. To do so, just type

dir

at the command line. You should be presented with a list of files and folders in your user folder - including the recognizable "Documents", "Downloads", "Music", "Pictures", and so on.

We need to run a command at the terminal to create a new Rails application, but we want to make sure we put it in a place that makes sense. You can create this application directly in your user folder if you like, but if you're planning on working on and playing around with more than one Rails application (and you should!) you probably want to go ahead and make a new folder. To make a folder called "dev" (short for development) in your user folder, type the command

mkdir dev

and hit enter.

If you run the "dir" command now, you should see all of the same folders as before, plus a new one, "dev". You can confirm that this folder exists in Windows Explorer - navigate to

C:\Users\YourUserName by going to My Computer, selecting the C drive, selecting the Users folder, and then selecting your name, or by opening your Documents and navigating up a level (in Windows 7, double click your user name in the "YourUserName > Documents" part of the window at the top). When you navigate to your user folder, you should see the same folders that were listed in the dir command, including the new "dev" folder.

We need to navigate to our new folder in order to run commands there. To do so, type

cd dev

at the terminal, and hit enter. "cd" stands for "change directory", and the argument is the directory you want to change to. Confirm that you're in the "dev" folder by observing that the prompt now reads C:\Users\YourUserName\dev>, and that running dir only shows two folders named "." and "..".

We're almost done with terminal shenanigans - for future reference, you should know that "." and ".." refer to the directory you're currently in, and the directory above it, respectively. If you want to move from the dev folder back to your user folder, you could type

cd C:\Users\YourUserName

and hit enter, which would move you to that folder. Or, you could just type *cd ..*

and hit enter, since ".." refers to the directory above the current directory, and that directory is the user directory. Go ahead and try the "cd .." command, run "dir" to confirm you're in your user directory, and then move back to your dev folder with "cd dev".

When you're in your dev folder, you're ready to create a new rails project. Run the command (by typing at the command line and pressing enter)

rails new myprojectname

with "myprojectname" replaced by your project's name (if you don't have one, just call it "test"). Rails will execute a few commands, but when it is done, there should be a new "myprojectname" folder in your dev folder. You can confirm this by opening your dev folder in Windows Explorer or running the dir command.

At this point, the only thing left to do is start your Rails server. Switch to the newly-created "myprojectname" directory (run the command cd myproject name from the dev folder). There, run the command

rails server

This will start your development server. You can access it by pointing your web browser at the URL http://localhost:3000. If the output of "rails server" gives an error telling you to run "bundle install", then do so - just type bundle install at the command line and hit enter, and let the program run. When it's done, go ahead and run rails server again.

Note that you need to leave your terminal open in order to keep the rails server running. To edit any of the scripts, you'll want to use a programmer's text editor. Notepad++ (available from notepad-plus-plus.org) is a great choice.

In particular, since Rails is normally deployed on Unix based computers (running Linux or Mac OSX), the files that Rails generate use Linux line endings - if you open them in Notepad, they'll appear to only have one line. If you open the files using Notepad++, it'll automatically detect the correct line ending format and everything will appear correctly.

Note that a text editor is *not the same as a word processor*: you don't want to use Microsoft Word or Libre Office to write code, as code can't have any of the formatting information that Word has to include.

Connecting to MySQL

As of now, you have a full-fledged Ruby on Rails installation, but you aren't connected to the MySQL database - instead, Rails is using an internal, lightweight database called SQLite.

First, installing MySQL support on Windows requires the expanded Ruby Development Kit. Go to http://rubyinstaller.org/downloads

and under the "Other Useful Downloads" section find the link for "DevKit-tdm-XXX.exe", where the "XXX" is a bunch of numbers.

To enable MySQL, you need to install the MySQL gem. Rails makes this really easy - just edit the file "Gemfile" in your application directory and add a new line

gem 'mysql2'

near any one of the other "gem xxxx" lines. Then, after you've saved the file, run "bundle install" on the command line in the application folder (go ahead and kill the server you started with "rails server" by hitting Ctrl and C first). Running "bundle install" makes sure that all the gems that are listed in your Gemfile are installed and up-to-date, so it will now install the MySQL connector gem.

The last thing to do is tell Rails where it can access the MySQL database. From the application folder, find the "config" sub folder, and open the file "database.yml" with your text editor.

Now that we've got a development environment setup, we're ready to actually build an application.

Building an Application

Note that in order to prototype and build an application, you must have a development environment setup. Refer to the previous section if you don't already have a working installation of WordPress or Rails.

Note that in order to do truly novel stuff in WordPress or almost anything in Rails, you'll need to know to to program in PHP or Ruby, respectively. This guide won't teach you how to program - better teachers have already published better resources elsewhere. There are many free tutorials on the internet, which you should be able to jump right into into since you already have PHP or Rails setup.

Tizag.com has a great series of tutorials on PHP that require no previous experience. For Ruby, check out Chris Pine's "Learn to Program" tutorials (http://pine.fm/LearnToProgram/) - he wrote an excellent book that you can buy from The Pragmatic Programmer, or you can access the orginal tutorials the book is based on for free in the left-hand bar of the site. Once you understand Ruby, you can move on to learning the specifics of Rails, which isn't very hard at all. There are several great tutorials out there - in particular, any content published by Ryan Bates at railscasts.com is guaranteed to be excellent.

It might also be useful to learn the basics of how JavaScript works - make sure you make use of the jQuery (http://jquery.org) library.

If you want to build a complex application, there is no way to skip out on learning a little programming. But you can save a lot of effort by making use of public libraries that have been published by others - WordPress plugins and themes, Rails gems, and HTML templates.

Wordpress Plugins and Themes

With Wordpress there is a plugin or theme for almost any situation that you can imagine, the best way to approach a wordpress site is, in fact, to think about what kind of look and what kinds of functionality will be most useful to you and then use Google to search for the themes and plugins that fit the ticket.

If, for example, you want to create a website to sell your new line of t-shirts, there are many great e-commerce themes available for Wordpress. To find the "best" one, a good place to start would be to search "Best eCommerce Theme Wordpress" in Google. Better yet, if you search, "Best eCommerce Theme Wordpress [Year]" in Google you are sure to find the themes that take advantage of the latest advances in Wordpress' already stellar platform.

Plugins work similarly -- there are shopping carts, survey, photo gallery, membership, gamification, forum, and mailing list plugins for Wordpress along with literally thousands of others. I am not exaggerating when I say that if there is a basic web function that you need, there is likely a free and easy to use Wordpress plugin to make it happen. This abundance of choice is also one of Wordpress' greatest downsides, there are so many plugins that you can't always be certain what is good, that's why when selecting plugins, your best bet is almost always to find two. Why? Because often you'll find one that works significantly better than the other for your needs.

As for paying for themes and plugins, the rule of thumb with themes is that you should only pay for one if you absolutely, positively love the theme and can't find anything similar among the thousands of free choices. This can include cases when you wish to use one of the many great Wordpress theme frameworks like Thesis or Genesis (frameworks are like lego kits for Wordpress themes, and they allow you to make custom themes without knowing how to program). This rule is doubly so as it relates to plugins, usually the only plugins you'll need to pay for are ones with direct commercial applications, and even then most of the good plugin providers will give you a free option to allow you to try before you buy.

Other HTML Themes

Wordpress is great in part because of the multitude of plug-and-play themes that are available for it. However, it you're developing a site that isn't based on wordpress - including a site based on Rails - a wordpress theme won't help you very much. However, there are some useful starting points available.

In particular, it is worth checking out a CSS package called 960gs (for "960 grid system"), available for download at http://960.gs. 960.gs provides a couple of CSS files that you can include on your HTML page to make grids really easy. Check out the demo file that is included in the 960.gs download to learn how to use it. Once you have a grid set up, you can add CSS classes to each box you want to style, and easily change its appearance.

One of the big trends in design is something called "responsive design" - instead of creating two websites, one for mobile devices and one for desktop and laptop computers, you only create one website, with one theme, that "responds" to the user's screen size. 960.gs isn't responsive, but you can make it so - one great adaptation of the 960gs system that adds responsiveness is called Unsemantic, and can be downloaded at http://unsemantic.com.

Rails Gems

One of the main benefits of Rails is that there are numerous code libraries (called "gems") available for it. You can and should make use of these libraries to make your project come together quicker - if someone else has already written a library to do something, why should you duplicate their effort?

There are thousands of rails gems available, that do all sorts of things for your website. In general, before writing a part of your application, take a second to think - is the feature I'm about to write on a lot of websites? Is it even on a few websites? If it is, there's probably a gem that does it for you. A quick google search for "rails gem + your feature here" will probably turn up something useful.

Another great resource to discover new gems is http://railscasts.com, a rails video tutorial series by Ryan Bates. Unfortunately, most of the new RailsCasts material requires a $9/mo subscription to view, but all of it is of the highest quality. Even if you don't subscribe, look at the titles of the videos he posts, and their short descriptions - if a gem is featured on RailsCasts, it is assured to be of high quality and worth your consideration.

Here, we'll just list a handful of gems that you should seriously consider using for your application. You should be able to find tutorials on how to use them - or any other gem - easily.

Paperclip: Paperclip is a file uploading gem that allows you to easily add a file field to a class and create form elements for the file. It also includes different ways to validate the file, including limiting files that are uploaded by size, file extension, and so on. Check it out if you will need to let users upload files to your application.

Will Paginate: Will Paginate lets you easily take output that might have many lines and paginate it, so the user only views the first X results, and has links to pages 2 or more. If your application is going to show list-based output of unspecified length, you will want to consider this gem - it makes it a lot easier to keep your design manageable, since you won't have to worry about displaying ten-thousand-element lists.

Delayed Job: Most of the time, all the processing that has to be done on a web application is fast and easy. Create a new user - takes maybe 50 milliseconds. Search for a post- perhaps 100ms. But some applications crunch some serious data, and need to be able to run processes that take longer than the maximum time to return a webpage. If you need to do this, you should check out Delayed Job, which provides a mechanism for spawning and managing background processes for your application.

Devise: There's a good chance your application will want to allow people to log in and out of it, and create an account for that purpose. Devise handles this, and more. In addition to providing a secure way to handle acocunts, it will allow you to let your users log in with Facebook, Google, and Twitter easily. Setting up these systems is still somewhat complex, even with Devise, but it is much easier with Devise than without. As a bonus, Devise also can handle email confirmations for your users and other common log-in tasks.

Part 2
Easy Mode: WordPress on a VPS

For some projects, especially ones without too much custom functionality, WordPress by itself is a perfectly acceptable option. If you just want to set up a website with WordPress, you don't need to jump through quite as many hoops, as you don't need to configure your own server from the bottom up. The first steps - obtaining a domain name and understanding how to set nameservers - are the same, though. It's worth at least reading through this section even if you intend to set up a full Ruby on Rails environment later.

Wordpress

Wordpress is magical.

For the non-programmer, there is almost no better way to begin a web project. The reason is simple, Wordpress is the lego set of web development, with thousands of plugins, tens of thousands of templates, and hundreds of thousands of man hours poured into making it user friendly for developers, designers, and weekend tinkerers alike.

To understand this point you need to get past a common misconception, that Wordpress is strictly a "blogging platform". That if you aren't putting up a personal journal, Wordpress has nothing for you. This couldn't be more incorrect. Strictly speaking, Wordpress is a Content Management System (CMS), and falls into the same category as other CMS' like Drupal, Joomla and Sitepoint. Wordpress alone powers 22% of all new websites (as of 2011) and has been downloaded over 65 million times. Why the popularity? It part it's because for years Content Management Systems have been the go to software platform for building web projects great and small, because unlike flat websites built in HTML and CSS they are database driven, with well designed administration panels which allow you to add posts, pages, navigation elements and functionality across the entire site on the fly.

In addition, the community that develops using Wordpress is absolutely enormous and building on its simple architecture, they have created plugins for almost any occasion. Do you want to build a fully functional store-front? There is a plugin for that. A Social Network? There is a plugin for that. A paid membership site? Sure there is a plugin for that. These are just the most obvious options, with the creative combination of plugins and widgets the sky is the limit.

Wordpress is a lego set and like all lego sets, to get the most out it the first thing you need to do is get organized. This section of the guide will help you do just that. First we will describe how to setup your development environment, then we will introduce you to templates, plugins and some of the things you'll need to get started with Wordpress. Finally, we'll dig a little deeper into the file system and show you how, with almost no programming ability whatsoever, you can customize the look and feel of your Wordpress site.

The Domain Name

Important Note - In the following sections we refer to several tasks (setting up a database, sftp, file transfers, and name server configuration) that are web host specific. We describe the processes generally here, but for your convenience we have provided links to specific instructions for several major web hosts.

Before we do anything else, you will need a domain name. There are literally thousands of options available for buying domains, but for the purposes of this introduction we will assume that you went with GoDaddy. Why GoDaddy? GoDaddy's advantage lies in its size and cost. Size because it is one of the largest domain registrars in the business, so it's unlikely that it will disappear tomorrow leaving your domain name in limbo. Cost because as a large registrar it's incredibly easy to find a discount code that will bring your first year domain costs down to $6-7. If you have trouble tracking one of these codes down for yourself, the best of them are usually available at RetailMeNot (retailmenot.com).

Once you've purchased your domain, there is only one thing you need to know about how it functions to get Wordpress zipping along, and that's how to change the name server.

What in the heck is a name server? To understand that, first recall our discussion of DNS earlier and then let's take a quick peek under the hood of your domain. The first thing that you'll notice is that a domain name is little more than that, a name, an alias for the website's "real" address. It is a human readable version of the IP address of the server on which the website resides.

Think of an IP address like you would your street address, it is the precise location of your house (website) relative to every other house (website) in the world. A domain name then is like giving someone directions by telling them to come to "John's house" rather than 555 NW Maple Drive. It's far easier to remember and often more descriptive than rattling off the address itself.

Take Google for example, to get to Google you have two choices -- first, you can go to your web browser and type "google.com" into the address field, fractions of a second later you will be treated to Google's iconic search bar. Alternatively, you can type 74.125.224.227 into the same bar. This is Google's IP address. Both take you to the same place, one is just a whole lot easier to remember.

A name server then is a system that maps your domain name to your IP address. Most web hosts have their own, unique name servers and you will need to know them along with how to change the default ones currently connected to your domain name in order to "move" it to your new host. Nameservers are usually structured something like this -- NS3.DOMAINNAME.COM and you will usually have anywhere between 2 and 5 of them (NS3.DOMAINNAME.COM, NS4.DOMAINNAME.COM, NS5.DOMAINNAME.COM, etc...). To change your name server in GoDaddy, simply click on products, domain management, your domain, and set nameservers, then enter the new name servers given to you by your web host. To change your name server in any other domain registrar, do a quick google search or contact your registrars customer service.

Finding a Web Host

Once you have a domain name, you will need to find a web host. Later in this guide, we will show you how to setup your own server using Amazon, however, for now we will assume that you are purchasing a shared hosting solution or a Virtual Private Server (VPS). The differences between the two revolve around the amount of computing resources you will have access to. Shared hosting plans usually involve your website being hosted alongside many other websites on the same server, you share that servers resources and its IP address -- this is often the cheapest option, and is perfect for small, personal websites or applications. A Virtual Private Server (VPS) provides you with a "slice" of a servers computing resources, partitioned off from a more powerful machine. Because you have exclusive access to these resources, you can treat a VPS like an independent server, with its own IP address and file system. A VPS is usually appropriate for large personal projects or very small commercial ones, and can be seamlessly scaled up as more resources become necessary.

Setting up your hosting solution is hugely dependent on the host that you choose, and can usually be completed in an afternoon. The most important things you'll need to figure out is how to get access to your server's file system through SFTP and how to get access to your hosts cPanel so that you can manage your domains and setup a database.

SFTP

It's now time to download your first piece of software, WinSCP (winscp.net). WinSCP is a File Transfer Protocol (FTP) and Secure File Transfer Protocol (SFTP) client for the Windows operating system. Before we get too much deeper, let's take a moment to understand what FTP and its secure cousin is.

FTP is the most common protocol used to transfer files from one one host to another, SFTP is an encrypted version of the standard FTP protocol that allows for secured transfer. An FTP client like WinSCP allows you to access your host (server) and transfer files to and from it. It's easiest to think of your web host like the file system of your computer, with directories and subdirectories. Normally, it is not possible to "see" these files from your web browser, however, a FTP client allows you to do so. We will need this in order to transfer the Wordpress files to your server.

When you are first setting up WinSCP it will ask you for a few pieces of information, all of which you can get from your web host:

- **Host Name:** This is the IP address of your server.
- **Port Number:** Usually the default (22) will be fine.
- **User Name:** This is the username, given to you by your host, to access your server.
- **Password:** Self explanatory
- **Private Key:** Sometimes, your host will provide you with a file called a private key. This is an additional layer of security. If your host has given you a key, this is where you put it.

Finally, from the File Protocol drop-down menu select SFTP if it is not already selected by default.

If everything went well, you should be logged into your server into a few seconds.

Setting Up Your Database

Before digging around in your file system, let's setup a MYSQL database.

SQL stands for structured query language, and speaks to the scripting language used to query a structured database. A database is what separates a flat website made from HTML and CSS from a dynamic web application. A database allows web software to store data, retrieve data and manipulate data generated by your website. In the case of Wordpress, the database is where all of your posts, pages, plugins, preferences, users, and everything else that can change dynamically will be stored.

There are many kinds of database software in use today (NOSQL, PostgreSQL, MongoDB) but by far the most common and well known is MYSQL. In a shared hosting environment or a VPS, databases are most commonly created in a piece of software called a cPanel (or VirtualMin). Since the control panel you get is dependent on your host, from here forward I will simply refer to them collectively as "cPanels". When you sign up for your web host you should be given a username and password to access your cPanel along with a web address where your cPanel is installed. For shared hosts, this is usually somewhere on your host's server, for VPS' it is often stuctured as http://yourdomainname.com:xxxxx where the x's are numbers (often 10000). Once you are logged into your cPanel your first mission is to setup a new MYSQL database to store your Wordpress data. Often, before this, you will also need to add your domain to your cPanel so that it can create a directory for it on your server. Whether or not you need to do this will be discussed in your host's documentation.

Creating a new database can be as simple as finding and clicking on the MYSQL Database Server link in your cPanel (locations will vary) and then clicking on "Create New Database". Name your database something that you will remember, and leave the rest of the options (such as character set) as their defaults.

Databases require "users" in order to be used. A user is an object with permission to access and manipulate the information inside the database. The menu to create users can usually be found in the same place that you found the menu to create a new database, the important thing is to make sure you set a password and leave the rest of the settings in their default positions.
Take note of your database name, username and password, you will need all of this information to install Wordpress.

Installing Wordpress

Finally we are ready to install Wordpress. The first thing you need to do is download the latest version of the software from wordpress.org. Once downloaded, unzip it into a directory you'll remember and open up WinSCP.

If you haven't done so already, it's time to add your web host's details to WinSCP. Click "New" and add your host name, username, password and private key (if you have one) as described above.

When you're finished you should be able to login to your servers file system. At this point, what you do next depends on whether you are using a shared hosting environment or a VPS. Usually with shared hosting environments you will be taken straight to the directory containing your website's files (which should be mostly empty). From here you might see a folder called "public_html", this is where Wordpress' files will be placed. Once again, this might differ slightly, if you have any confusion about where to put your files in a shared hosting environment please contact your web host.

In a VPS you will most likely be taken to your "root" directory. Remember that a VPS is really a slice of a server, and thus you have access to the entire file system of that server rather than just the directory in which your website is stored. From the root directory, find the folder labeled "home," from there click on the directory containing your website (you may have set this in your "cPanel" earlier). Once there, find the public_html folder just as you would in a shared hosting environment.

Now all you have to do is drag and drop all the files from inside of the Wordpress folder into the public_html directory of your server. After a few moments you will be done. Finally, visit your domain name and follow the onscreen instructions, adding your database and database user name and password along with any other information Wordpress requests. After a few more moments of installation you will have a fully functioning Wordpress install -- congratulations!

Themes and Plugins

The latest versions of Wordpress make it really easy to upload themes and plugins from right inside of your administration panel, but what's the fun in that? To really get a feeling for how your Wordpress install works, we need to spend a bit more time in WinSCP and learn about the file system that Wordpress uses. To begin, let's learn how to install a new theme.

Picking a Theme

Finding a theme is as easy as doing a Google search, there are hundreds of thousands of them available for just about any occasion. Moreover, there are tens of thousands of Top Ten lists to show you the best ones for your situation.

The easiest way I've found to find a theme is this --

1. Decide what kind of website I want to build (e.g. An eCommerce site)
2. Search "Best Wordpress eCommerce Theme [Year]"
3. Scan the results until I find something I like.

Many people immediately rush to purchase a theme, I've found that this is usually unnecessary if you are willing to take some time. There are so many free themes available out there, that unless you have very specific needs you should be able to find something that you can work with.

If you do decide to buy a theme, you should definitely take a look at elegantthemes.com, they offer 81 (at the time of writing) fantastic themes for $39 a year. It's easily the best deal I've ever found.

Once you find a theme, installing it is just as easy as installing Wordpress itself. Open up WinSCP, go into the wp_content/themes folder of your Wordpress directory, drag and drop the files (directory and all) into the directory and voila, your new theme will be ready to go in the administration panel of Wordpress.

Installing a plugin

Same story, different day. The process of finding and installing a plugin is very similar to the process of installing a theme. The only difference is where the plugin ultimately goes, the wp_content/plugins folder rather than the wp_content/themes folder.

Finally the File System

So you want to change the way that your Wordpress theme operates? While many modern themes have comprehensive administration panels which will give you the ability to change the look and feel of your theme, it's nice to have at least some idea of how the file system works so that if you are ever interested in moving things around for yourself, you know where to start. Below is a listing of the files that control the layout of your theme, and what they usually contain. We highly recommend that you open these up and experiment with them in WinSCP. While a basic understanding of HTML would be extremely valuable, it is not necessary, as a bit of tinkering and few page refreshes should give you a good idea of what each line does. Generally anything not wrapped in a <?php ?> tag is safe to fiddle with. Everything inside those tags is written in PHP and will often have a profound impact on the way that your theme operates. As always, user discretion is advised.

Just in case, be certain to have a clean copy of your theme on hand in case things go to awry.

All of your themes files can be found in wp_content/themes/[theme-name]

header.php - Header usually contains everything above the fold, including your sites navigation elements (if it includes a top nav). Header is also where you will find all of your themes HTML Meta Tags, and so is the most common place to put tags that need to appear site-wide (e.g. Google Analytics)

index.php - This file contains everything that you see when your site first loads, including Wordpress' main loop (the programming loop that controls how posts are displayed). Index.php is also used to "call" the sidebar and the footer. If you delete those calls (usually found at the end of the file) your sidebar and/or footer will quickly disappear alongside it. You might also see a file called home.php, in those cases your theme creator has chosen to overwrite the default index.php behavior and provide a custom homepage template.

single.php - This file contains what each of your blog posts will look like. If you are using Wordpress as a blog this is where you can change how it is laid out. It is broken up similarly to the index but on a smaller scale, with the posts header (usually containing the date, author and number of comments), the post's content and then the posts footer (usually containing the comments section).

page.php - This file contains how your non-blog pages will look like, very similar to single.php. Using Wordpress' templating system you can make your own custom page templates to do just about anything that you could want.

sidebar.php - This file contains all the information that drives the sidebar(s) of your site. Since so many Wordpress themes have been widgetized, unless you have a custom bit of code you are interested in placing in the sidebar it is likely best to make changes in the Wordpress administration panel.

footer.php - This file contains everything located in your website's footer and is a great spot to put any custom tracking code you might wish to install. This is another section of the theme that has been highly widgetized and may be best managed through the administration panel.

What About Style.css?

That's an excellent question that we can only answer once we understand what a Cascading Style Sheet (the .css in style.css) is.

A Cascading Style Sheet is the document that contains all the styling and layout information for a web page. It tells the browser not only how every font, bullet, and text block should look but also controls the overall layout of the page -- from how far apart the letters should be spaced, to how wide the columns should be.

As websites have become more sophisticated, CSS has taken on a host of new tasks, including handling many cross-browser support issues and allowing for fancy onscreen effects like drop shadows.

There are hundreds of good guides on developing using CSS, but for our purposes all we want you to do is to be able to recognize when it is being used, what it might be doing and how to make minor adjustments.

class and id

When you look at any of the files listed above, you are almost certain to run into an HTML tag. These tags are usually structured like this -- <[xxx] > [information of some kind] </[xxx]>. Where the x's can be anything from "img" which places an image to "strong" which turns the text within it bold to "h1" which makes the text a large headline. The catalog of html tags is mind boggling, and if you are interested I would suggest stepping through the very decent tutorial on W3 School (http://www.w3schools.com/html/default.asp).

Now the question you may have is how does the browser know how large to make the h1 headline, and moreover how does it know what font to use in making it, that's where CSS comes into play.

Let's say we want to have a headline for the title of our webpage that says, "Really Cool Webpage," and we want to make the font green and 26px high. To do this we have two choices, the first is using only HTML:

`<h1 style="font-size: 26px; color: green;">Really Cool Webpage</h1>`

This works like a charm, now you have a 26px high green Really Great Website sitting wherever you place this little snippet of HTML. This, however, isn't very efficient. What if you want all of your headlines to be 26px high and green? In that case you would be forced to type out this inline style information every single time that you need it. Not only is this a huge pain, but it opens up significant opportunities for errors.

CSS provides us with an answer, by allowing us to define a set of behaviors in a separate file and call on those behaviors within the document we need them. In our previous example, if you looked at your Wordpress page and decided that you wanted all of your headlines to be green and 26px high you would open up style.css and search for "h1".

More than likely you will see a listing that looks something like this:

```
h1{
  margin: 10px 0 20px;
  font-size: 24px;
  color: blue;
  font-weight: normal;
  text-transform: uppercase;
  letter-spacing: .05em;
```

word-spacing: .2em;
}

For now, the only two lines that matter to you are "font-size" and "color". To get the headline that you want, you would change font-size to 26px and color to green. Now, when you refresh your blog every place where the h1 tag is called you will now have a slightly bigger, slightly greener version instead.

What if you only want a small subset of h1's to have this behavior? This is where classes and id's come into place. These are snippets of behavior you can call on when you need them. The differences between them are a bit confusing, but boil down to this -- you use an id when you want to control a single HTML element, such as h1. You use a class when you wish to control multiple HTML elements, for example, h1 and p.

To make the changes above using classes or ids, we can add one of two pieces of code to the style.css file:

#idname { color: green, font-size: 26px; }

OR

.classname (color: green, font-size: 26px; }

Now we open up any file containing h1's we wish to style this way and alter them as follows to call on the style:

<h1 id="idname">Really Cool Website</h1>

OR

<h1 class="classname">Really Cool Website</h1>

CSS can be used for thousands and thousands of minor alterations to your web page, for a good starters guide to introduce you to some of the changes you can make, we highly suggest stepping through a few of the CSS examples at W3 School (http://www.w3schools.com/css/default.asp)

Inspect Element and Experimentation

Understanding how the CSS on your site works can be a daunting task, fortunately if you are using Google's Chrome browser, it can be made much easier by taking advantage of the Inspect Element option in the left-click drop down menu. If you want to know which styles are affecting a particular area of your site, simply left click on that area, select "Inspect Element" and then a panel will appear showing you all the style data associated with it and even the line in style.css that style data resides. You can even change this data on the fly to see what the site will look like if you were to alter something. These changes will be reversed the next time that you load the page, but it is still a really good way to experiment with CSS without risk of messing anything up on a live site.

Part 3

Hard Mode: Building from Scratch

Using Amazon's Web Services

For this part of the guide, we're going to use Amazon's cloud service. There are several reasons for this - one, Amazon's Web Services has a full suite of tools that enable you to deploy all sorts of hardware as a service quickly and easily, including servers, load balancers, network drives, and so on. It is a solution that scales with your application - as your website grows, it takes just minutes to scale AWS up to your needs. Plus, it's cheap - I have been using AWS for at least two years now and have seen them lower their prices at least once a quarter.

For everything you use on AWS, you are billed for your usage. If you start a "small" server, run it for one hour, and then turn it off, you are billed for 1 hour of "small" server usage - at the time of writing, six cents. If you use 10 gb of hard drive space for 1 month, you're billed $0.10 /gigabyte - a total of a dollar for the month. The incremental costs are incredibly low, so if you want to experiment, you should feel free to do so.

The other major benefit is that when you sign up for AWS, you get a "free usage tier" for 1 year. This enables you to use a "Micro" sized server, 10 gigabytes of storage, and as much bandwidth as you'll probably need for free for a year. If you go over the "free usage tier", you will be billed, but at very reasonable rates - you'd have to rack up a bill more than about $5 without starting a larger server.

The "Micro" sized server is great for development, or hosting a small website that doesn't see much traffic. It won't do much for you for hosting a web application, unless the application is very small and doesn't get a lot of traffic. You can follow this tutorial with any sized instance - we suggest Micro, since it's the cheapest. When you want to take your site live, you can upgrade the instance easily - without having to reconfigure anything, and only a minute of downtime - to a larger one.

Note that if you're going to be hosting a website 24x7, Amazon has "reserved" instances available. These charge you a non-refundable up-front fee, but have the advantage of much lower hourly rates. If you're going to be running a server 24x7 (like a web server), you can save up to 70% this way.

Before you move on, you need to sign up for AWS at http://amazon.com/aws. Click the "Sign Up" link in the top-left bar and follow the instructions. You'll need a credit card, but there is no charge until you've actually used something beyond the one-year free tier that you get for signing up. Nothing in this tutorial will go beyond the 1-year free tier, so if you just follow this, you won't be billed at all.

Setting up the Operating System

When you've signed up for AWS, you'll need to log in to the AWS console. There, there should be a link to "EC2". EC2, which stands for "Elastic Compute Cloud", is where you spin up instances - servers in the cloud.

To create your first instance, click on the EC2 link. You'll be taken to the EC2 dashboard, which should provide some information about how many and what type of instances are running. Click on "Instances" in the left hand bar to be taken to the instance view. Right now, you have no running instances, so there isn't much to see, but it should show the table that will populate as you launch servers.

Let's create your first instance. Click the "Launch Instance" button on the top part of the page. You'll be asked to choose a wizard - go ahead and select "Classic Wizard" and continue.

The first step in the wizard is to choose an AMI - an Amazon Machine Image - which will serve as the basis for your new instance. This is a copy of an entire server's data, stored in the cloud - when you choose an AMI and start an instance, a new copy is made, connected to a server, and turned on. It comes with the operating system already installed, so you can get started quickly.

For our operating system, we're going to use a version of Linux. Linux is a free and open source operating system that is widely used for servers. It has a lot of benefits, but the chief benefit for us is price and ease of getting help online. Since a lot of server software is written for Linux, it's easy to get started on it.

There are many different "flavors" of linux, called distributions. There are small differences between each one, but the core concepts are the same. We're going to use Ubuntu Linux 12.04. There are a couple of small downsides for using Ubuntu, but there are big upsides - if you're going to use Linux on your personal computer (which you should seriously consider!), Ubuntu or its sister versions Xubuntu and Lubuntu make great beginner Linux systems, so you only need to learn the details of one distribution.

Second, Ubuntu is very widely used. It's one of the most popular operating systems, so getting help online for it is easy. The wide adoption and ease of getting help makes life a lot easier.

On the AMI list shown, there should be a "Ubuntu Server 12.04 LTS" box. Go ahead and make sure the "64-bit" radio button next to it is checked, and then click "Select".

The next screen lets you choose how many instances (servers) to launch, and where to launch them. Amazon AWS resources are divided into "availability zones" - basically, data centers - and resources in the same availability zone can connect to each other much more quickly (and cheaply). You don't need to worry about which availability zone you choose (us-east-1b, us-east-1c, or us-east-1d are good choices), but you should remember which one you choose and make sure you deploy all resources to that zone in the future.

For now, go ahead and let the "Instance Type" field be "T1 Micro", unless you want to launch a larger (and more expensive) server. For the number of instances, leave it at the default of 1. Go ahead and "Continue".

On the next screen, go ahead and check the checkbox that says "Protect against accidental termination". Everything else can be left as a default. Select "Continue".

On the next screen, you'll be asked to configure your storage devices. For now, the defaults are fine - but when you want to host a real server for a large application, you may want to edit the "EBS Volume Size" to be greater than 8 gigabytes. An EBS volume is just a cloud version of a hard drive - for now, we're going to create a server with 8 GB of storage, which is enough to get a web server up and running, but may not be enough to host a large application. Go ahead and continue.

The next screen will let you name your server. The tech world has a long tradition of giving servers cool or funny names. Pick something that you'll remember, enter it in the "value" field next to the tag "Name", and continue.

There are just two more steps: creating a key pair so that we can remotely access the server, and setting up the firewall. On the current screen, there should be a radio button for "Create a new Key Pair" - select it if it isn't already selected. Enter a name for your keypair (I usually use the servername with "-key" added, like "algorithmi-key") and click "Create and download your key pair". **Save the file you download somewhere where you can find it!** You *cannot* download the key again from Amazon, and if you lose the key, it will be incredibly difficult to access the server. If you can, back it up in a couple of other places. The file that's downloaded will be the name you entered ".pem".

Once you've saved the key, continue. The last configuration screen asks you to create a security group and set permissions - Amazon Web Services comes with a firewall by default, and this will let you configure it. Go ahead and create a new security group, and then add new TCP/IP rules to allow inbound traffic on ports 22, 80, and 3000. Once that is done, continue.

The final screen will ask you to review the selections you've made and confirm if they are correct. Compare the listed settings and make sure they look correct, then click "Launch". Note that if something is wrong, it's simple to change the settings later using the web interface, or to terminate and create a whole new instance if necessary. You'll be billed only for what server time you use, to the nearest hour.

Once you confirm the instance launch, a new row should appear on the "Instances" screen with the newly created instance. It will take a minute, possible two, to start the first time. When the yellow dot next to "initializing" becomes a green dot next to "2/2 checks passed", the instance is up and running.

You'll now want to associate an IP address with this server. On the AWS dashboard, find the link to "Elastic IPs". Click it, and find the button on the top bar to "Allocate New Address". Click it, press "Yes, Allocate", and wait until a new row appears in the elastic IP listing. Once it does, right click on the address and click "Associate", and select your instance from the resulting menu. Confirm this. After you do, the "Instance ID" field in the elastic IP listing should change. Now you can access your server from that IP address.

Remote Access

Once the server instance you created is shown as "running" in the AWS management console, you'll want to do something with it. Right now, though, you haven't installed any software, so even if you type in the IP address for the server into your browser, it won't respond. We want to log into the server remotely so we can install software and setup our web server.

To connect, we'll use a protocol called SSH (which stands for **S**ecure **Sh**ell). SSH comes standard with Linux and Mac OSX, but not on

Windows, so we'll need to use a program called PuTTY. Find the "putty.exe" link at

http://www.chiark.greenend.org.uk/~sgtatham/putty/download.html

(or just google "Putty download", it'll be the first result) and save it to your desktop. Also grab the file "puttygen.exe". PuTTY doesn't actually have to be "installed" in the traditional sense to run - just double click the .exe file you downloaded and go.

You'll need the key file you downloaded from Amazon to connect to the server - using a key file to connect, while less convenient to set up than using a password, is much more secure and removes the need for you to remember yet another password.

First we have to convert the format of the key file. Open PuTTYGen. Click "Load", and find the key file you downloaded from Amazon, which ends in ".pem". When it is opened, PuTTYGen will import it to the PuTTY format. Click "Save Private Key" and save it somewhere you'll remember it.

Now open PuTTY. In the left bar, expand the "SSH" option, near the bottom, then select the "Auth" section by clicking on it. On the right hand side, find the button "Browse" next to the blank file path box. Click it, and navigate to the .ppk file you just saved using PuTTYGen.

Then, click the "Session" header at the top of the left bar to return to the front page. Enter your IP address as the "Host", and click "Connect".

PuTTY wil take a moment to connect, and then ask you which user you want to log in as - type "ubuntu" and hit enter to log in as the default user, ubuntu. If everything goes as planned, you'll see a lot of output (nothing which says "login failed"), and you'll be greeted with the linux terminal on your new server.

Linux Crash Course

By now, you should have an instance running on EC2, and you should have confirmed that the server is running by seeing the green dot and "2/2 checks passed" message in the EC2 dashboard. In addition, you should have set up PuTTY to connect to your instance, set up your key file, and succeeded in connecting.

You now have a remote terminal connection to your new Linux server. We'll be using the terminal to perform all of our set up, which may be quite different from what you're used to. That said, it is certainly worth using, as SSH and the terminal are very powerful tools - you may even come to prefer the terminal to a graphical user interface for some applications.

In addition, you may not have used Linux before, which means there is a little bit of a learning curve. We'll give you a crash course (to borrow from Neal Stephenson, it's a "747 power-diving into your apartment" kind of crash) on the Linux terminal, which should be enough to let you follow this tutorial and read help files on the internet. If you're already familiar with Linux and the terminal, go ahead and skip this section.

The terminal, also called a command line, is the most basic interface with the computer. You type a command, the computer runs the command, and spits the text output back at you. There are no images, no graphics to speak of - and yet, the terminal is incredibly powerful. It's also incredibly lightweight, which makes it the perfect interface for a remote server. All you have to do to get the machine to start doing things is type a command and hit enter. To prove it to yourself, go ahead and run this command:

top

by typing "top" and hitting enter. The terminal should be replaced with the output of a program called "top", which is a lot like the Task Manager you may have seen in Windows. It'll show information about memory use and processor use by the processes running on your machine, and update that output live. Once you've seen it running, exit top by hitting "q". You should see the same "ubuntu@ip-X-Y-Z"> prompt that was displayed before.

You're probably used to the folder / subfolder / file stucture on Windows machines. Linux uses the same structure, with only cosmetic differences. Instead of a "C:\" drive that you're probably used to, with folders under it, Linux goes ahead and puts all the folders at the base. In addition, while Windows uses backslashes (\) to separate folders, Linux uses forward slashes (/).

The prompt you're shown at the terminal tells you (the terminal) is in the system's file structure, called the current directory. However, right now it probably isn't showing anything - only listing "ubuntu@-ip-X-Y-Z". This is because you're currently in your *home folder*, which for brevity is not shown at the terminal - if the current folder is any other folder, the path will be shown as a subpath from home or as a full path at the prompt.

Linux has a convenient feature called a "home" folder - that is, each user has a folder, called the home folder, that is a sub-folder of the root folder "/home". This is a good place for you to put any files you might need - it is analogous to your user folder on Windows, which is where your "Documents", "Music", "Pictures", "Videos" and so on folders are located. As an example, the full folder path for the folder you're currently in - the user "ubuntu"'s home folder - is /home/ubuntu. If you created a new user called "ted", his home folder would be in /home/ted.

When you run commands in the terminal, it is assumed that any file arguments passed to the command start at the current folder. So, if you are currently in the folder /home/ubuntu/ and want to run a command on files in the folder /home/ubuntu/newfolder called "a.txt" and "b.txt", you would run

<command> newfolder/a.txt newfolder/b.txt

(Of course, remove the "<" and ">" from "<command>", and replace it with the command you want to run). Since you're in "/home/ubuntu", the computer will append the path "newfolder/a.txt" and "newfolder/b.txt" to create the correct paths. If you just ran

<command> a.txt b.txt

the computer would complain that a.txt and b.txt do not exist, since it is looking for files with the full paths "/home/ubuntu/a.txt" and "/home/ubuntu/b.txt", which don't exist.

If you want to specify an absolute path - that is, a path that starts with the root of the file system - just prepend a "/" to the path. So "/home/ubuntu/newfolder/a.txt" is an absolute path - but "home/ubuntu/newfolder/a.txt" will look for a subfolder of the current folder called "home", with a subfolder called "ubuntu", and so on.

There are a couple of useful commands you should know. For

example, to view the folders and files in a given folder, run the command:

ls

at the terminal. By defualt, "ls" (short for "list") will show you the folders and subfolders in the current directory, but it can take arguments that will change this behavior. For example, to show the folders and files in the subfolder "subfolder", run:

ls subfolder

If you want to see more information, you can use the "-l" option, which shows additional information. If you also want to show hidden files, use the option -a. For example, to show both hidden files and additional information for a subfolder use:

ls -a -l subfolder

If you run this command, you'll see the directories "." and "..", and some folders and files that begin with a ".". In Linux, to hide a file, you start its name with a period - so the file ".hidden" is hidden but the file "nothidden" is not. Note that hiding has nothing to do with password protection or the like - hiding a file does not change who can view it - but only changes whether the files are shown by default by the "ls" command.

The cryptic-sounding directories "." and ".." are shortcuts for the current directory, and the directory above the current directory (the superdirectory), respecitvely. For example, if you're in hte user ubuntu's home folder, then

ls .

will list the files and folders in the current folder, "/home/ubuntu". But if you run

ls ..

will list the files and folders in the superdirectory, "/home".

Now that you can see where you are in the file system, it's useful to be able to change the current directory. The command to do so is "cd", which stands for "change directory". Change directory takes one argument, the directory you wish to move to. So, if you'd like to move to the directory "/home/ubuntu/newfolder/subfolder", you could type

cd /home/ubuntu/newfolder/subfolder

But if you're already in the home folder, you can go ahead and leave off the "/home/ubuntu", and just type

cd newfolder/subfolder

Alternatively if you're in a subfolder of subfolder - for example, your full path is currently "/home/ubuntu/newfolder/subfolder/secondsub", then you could move to "/home/ubuntu/newfolder/subfolder" by using the ".." shortcut for the super directory:

cd ..

Now that we can look around and move around, we would like to be able to change some files. To delete a file, use the "rm" command - it takes one or more files as an argument. To delete a file called "a.txt" in the current directory, run

rm a.txt

Note that to delete a folder, you have to use the "-r" option, which stands for "recursive". So, to delete the whole folder called "subfolder" in the current directory, run

rm -r subfolder

To move a file, use the "mv" command. It takes two arguments: the current path of the file and the new path of the file. For example to move "a.txt" to a subfolder called subfolder, run

mv a.txt subfolder/a.txt

You can rename a file or folder by runnning "mv" on it. Tp rename "a.txt" to "b.rxt", run

mv a.txt b.rxt

Finally, to copy a file, use the "cp" command. It also takes two arguments, the first being the location of the file you want to copy, and the second the path you wish to copy it to.

What about text editing? Your installation of ubuntu will come with a console-based text editor called "nano" which is very beginner-friendly.

If you are already familiar with text editing on the command line (using nano or another text editor like pico, vim, or emacs), then skip this next section

Editing with Nano

Editing with nano is straightforward. To edit a file or create a new file, just run the command

nano <filename>

So to open a file called "a.txt" run "nano a.txt". If the file exists, it will be opened, if it does not, it will be created as soon as you save the file. When you open a new file, you'll notice the bottom bar has a bunch of commands listed, each with a key code starting with "^", like "^X Exit". The "^" refers to the Ctrl key, so to exit, hit Ctrl+x. "Write out" means "save", so to save the file hit Ctrl+o. If you want to search, instead of hitting Ctrl+f for "find", hit Ctrl+w for "Where is".

Other than that, all you need to do is type. To move the cursor without editing, use the arrow keys. That's all there is to it. You may want to try writing a file, saving it (Ctrl+w), exiting (Ctrl+x), and then viewing it with less (run "less <filename>") and nano (run "nano <filename>").

Alternatively if you just want to view a text file you can use the "less" command. Just run *less filename*

to open a file called "filename", or replace "filename" with the path to the file you want to view. Less is very easy to use - you can scroll up and down using the arrow keys or j and k, or page up and page down. To quit, hit q. Less is great for viewing very large files, since it doesn't need to load the entire file into memory.

Now that we can create, move, view, and edit text files, it's time to control who can access those files. Linux has a full-featured, easy to use (once you get the hang of it) permissions system.

Each file and directory has a set of three permissions grantable on it, to each of three different groups. The permissions are read, write, and execute, which each corresponds to exactly what you'd expect. The permissions can be granted to the user who owns the file, the group that owns the file, or everyone. Each file, then, is owned by a user and a group.

Go ahead and create a text file called "a" (note that in Linux there is no need to have specific file extensions unless an application tha tis going to access the file requires it) by running "nano a", typing a few words, and saving with Ctrl+x

We can view the permissions on this file by running "ls -l". The results are shown on the left, with the format "drwxrwxrwx", with some or all characters replaced by "-". The first letter, d (or -) corresponds to if the file is a directory (d) or not (-). The next triplet of "rwx" corresponds to the owner's permissions to read (r) or not (-), write (w) or not (-), and execute (x) or not (-). The second triplet of "rwx" uses the same code, but for the group, and the third triplet for all other users. Note that the output of ls -l probably has "ubuntu ubuntu" written two columns to the right of the permissions code - this corresponds to the owner (ubuntu) and owner group (also ubuntu). By default, new files you create are owned by your user and your user group (which is the group with just your user in it).

You can change the permissions of a file by running "chmod". This command takes two arguments- the permission to change and the file to change it on. The first argument is a set of letters - a group for whom to change the permission for, one for grant or revoke, and a group for the permission to change.

The options for who to change the permission for are "u" for user (owner), "g" for group, or "o" for other. If no option is specified, the permission will be changed for everyone. The symbol for revoke is "-" and the symbol for grant is "+". The permission symbols are r,w, and x, as in the output of "ls -l".

That's a lot, so here are some examples:

"chmod u+x a" grants the owner the execute permission for the file "a".

"chmod g-r a" revokes the read permission for the group for the file "a".

"chmod +w a" gives everyone the write permission for the file "a".

"chmod "ug+x a" gives the user and group the execute permission for file "a".

If you want to change who owns a file, use the "chown" command (short for "change owner"). This has an easier format: the first argument is the user and group to change ownership to in the format user:group, and the second is the file or folder to change the permisison for. For example,

chown ubuntu:ubuntu a

sets the owner group of the file or directory "a" to "ubuntu".

All of this is well and good, but there is a caveat - there is a user, named "root" (referred to as the "superuser") which has the right to read, write, and execute *any* file in the file system, much like the "administrator" user on Windows. On occasion, we'll have to execute commands as the superuser, which we can do by pre-pending the command "sudo" to whatever we want to run. For example, to change the owner of a folder "subdirectory" to "tim" as the superuser, run the command

sudo chown tim:tim subdirectory

This is useful if your user doesn't have permission to modify the subdirectory.

If you just remember what we've gone over (or keep it handy to reference later) you should be more than capable of working with the terminal. One note, though - if you start a terminal application, you may end up wondering how to exit it and return to the terminal prompt.

Finally, let's install some software. You can have multiple terminal sessions running, connected to the same machine. So, you could open four copies of PuTTY and connect in all of them in order to do 4 different things as once. However, there is a better way, a program called "tmux".

Before we explain how to use tmux, we're going to install it. We can install software in Linux by using an application called a *package manager*. Package managers are brilliant inventions - they allow you to automatically download, configure, and install applications from the internet using just a single command. They are a bit like the "app stores" present in modern mobile operating systems, but far older and much more powerful, as a package manager can automatically install any other packages that a package you want to install requires.

On Ubuntu, the package manager is called "apt", so we'll install software using the command "apt-get". But first, we should update the package manager's software lists, so let's run

sudo apt-get update

This will show a lot of output as apt downloads new package lists from the ubuntu servers.

Tmux isn't installed by default, so to install it run the command

sudo apt-get install tmux

This will do a bit of processing and automatically install and configure tmux, or tell you that tmux is already installed. We're now ready to run tmux - just run the command "tmux".

When tmux starts, it'll add a new green frame to your terminal. Tmux is a *terminal multiplexer* - it lets you view multiple terminals on one screen, and switch between sets of terminals easily. It's also highly configurable and lets you re-access old terminal sessions from new PuTTY logins. As you can see, a terminal is already started, but let's open a new one. To give tmux a command, hit "Ctrl" and "b" (written as Ctrl+b), then type the keyboard shortcut for what you want to do.

Let's split the screen into two terminals. Hit Ctrl+b, then type %. This will split the terminal in two halves vertically. Only one pane will have a cursor - you can switch between them by hitting Ctrl+b and typing "o". You can do this while a program or command is executing in one terminal in order to multi-task.

We can also create whole new sets of panes. To do so, hit Ctrl+b and then "c". A new, single terminal will appear, and a "1-bash" will appear at the bottom bar, next to the already-existant "0-bash". Each of these refers to a set of panes, and the "*" next to "1-bash" indicates that you're viewing set 1. To switch between sets, use Ctrl+b n (to go forward 1), Ctrl+b p (to go back 1), or Ctrl+b N, where N is a number, to switch to a specific number. Try this now.

To close a terminal, just type "exit" at it. If a pane isn't responding and you need to kill it, type Ctrl+b x. This will ask you if you want to kill the pane - hit "y" to accept, or "n" to reject.

Finally, if you want to disconnect and reconnedt to your stored session, you can do so easily. Just close PuTTY, open a new session, and reconnect. When you've reconnected, type *tmux attach*

to access your old session, with the same windows and output stored.

We're finally ready to get started.

The Web Server

Note: In this section, we'll assume you have a basic familiarity with Linux. If you don't, go ahead and re-read the previous section, or at least keep it open for reference.

For our webserver, we're going to use nginx (pronounced "enigne x"). The most popular web server out there today is Apache, but nginx is very easy to configure, offers incredibly high performance, and is generally a good choice.

Note that you **should install as part of the rails deployment if you're using rails**. So, if you plan to set up rails, go ahead and skip to the "Ruby on Rails" section.

To install nginx, run

sudo apt-get install nginx

(When asked if you want to continue, press "y").

This will go ahead and install nginx for you. You can now start nginx by running

sudo service nginx start

If everything goes well, you'll be greeted by a "Starting nginx: nginx" message. You can now confirm that nginx is running by typing in your server's ip address into a browser. You should be greeted with a festive "Welcome to nginx!" message.

That's it! We'll have to configure nginx once we've got everything installed, but nginx is up and running successfully.

For future reference, you can stop nginx from running with

sudo service nginx stop

and you can make nginx restart with

sudo service nginx restart

That's all for now. Note that if you installed nginx using this method, your nginx path is /etc/nginx/, not /opt/nginx, and the configuration file is /etc/nginx/nginx.conf, not /opt/nginx/conf/nginx.conf. You'll need to adjust paths accordingly.

Let's move on to installing a database.

Databases

For now, we're going to use MySQL as our database. MySQL, though not the fastest or newest database around, is a good all-arounder that has good support for connecting to a lot of different software. Since it is a popular choice, it isn't hard to find support for it online. Install it by running the command

sudo apt-get install mysql-server

and confirming the installation when asked. The installer will ask you to set a root password - choose something secure! A good way to do so is to generate a random password, there are several random password generators online. Make sure you write the password down somewhere you'll remember; you'll need it later.

Once the installer is complete, you can confirm that you can test the connection to your MySQL server by running *mysql -u root -p*

and typing in the password you set earlier when prompted. If you're greeted by a "mysql>" prompt, MySQL is set up successfully. You can exit by typing "exit" into the mysql prompt and hitting enter.

There are other options for your database back end, including PostgreSQL, a popular alternative to MySQL, and NoSQL alternatives like MongoDB.

PHP and WordPress

NOTE: If you're planning on setting up rails, you should have installed nginx via the method suggested there. If you installed nginx as suggested in the "nginx" section, *then* installed it as suggested in rails as well, you'll have a couple of problems.

Recall that if you installed nginx using Rails, your nginx path is probably /opt/nginx/, and the nginx configuration file is located at /opt/nginx/conf/nginx.conf. If you installed using the package manager, your nginx directory is /etc/nginx, and the configuration file is /etc/nginx/nginx.conf.

Now that nginx and MySQL are installed, we need to install php, and the MySQL extensions for it. This is pretty straightforward. Run the command

sudo apt-get install php5-fpm php5-mysql

to install PHP5 and FPM, the bridge between PHP and web serves. When it's done, we need to configure nginx to connect to PHP. Open the nginx configuration file with the command

sudo nano /opt/nginx/conf/nginx.conf

(Remember to replace the path with "/etc/nginx/nginx.conf" if you installed nginx using apt-get)

and find the "server {" block. You can go ahead and delete the default one shown, complete from the opening "server {" to the matching closing brace }. Then, go ahead and create a new server block, making it look like this:

server {

    listen 80;

    server_name localhost;

    root /home/ubuntu/wordpress;

```
    index index.php;
    location / {
            try_files $uri $uri/ /index.php;
    }

    location ~ \.php$ {
            fastcgi_pass 127.0.0.1:9000;
            fastcgi_read_timeout 600;
            fastcgi_param SCRIPT_FILENAME $document_root$fastcgi_script_name;
            fastcgi_param SCRIPT_NAME $fastcgi_script_name;
            include /opt/nginx/conf/fastcgi_params;
    }
}
```

When you've made the required edits, save them, exit, and restart the nginx process with "sudo service nginx restart".

Now all we have to do is put the wordpress code in the right location, which we specified with the "root" directive as "/home/ubuntu/wordpress". You can download wordpress straight to your server from http://wordpress.org; just copy-paste the link from the "Download" link and use it with the wget command while in your home folder, like so:

wget http://wordpress.org/latest.zip

This will download the file from the server and save it as latest.zip. Now, unzip it, using the command

unzip latest.zip

The terminal may tell you that the program "unzip" is not installed. If it isn't, install it with the command "sudo apt-get install unzip".

If you instead download the .tar.gz version, use the command

tar -xvzf latest.tar.gz

There's just one last task to perform - set the group of the wordpress/directory to www-data, so that the web server can access it. Do this with the command

sudo chown -R ubuntu:www-data wordpress/

(The -R option makes it recursive, i.e., all subdirectories are also re-owned). For good measure, restart php-fpm and nginx with the commands

sudo service nginx restart

sudo service php5-fpm restart

Try visiting your website by typing the IP address you assigned in EC2 into a browser. With any luck, you'll see the wordpress configuration screen. From here, you have a fully functioning WordPress environment, so you can follow the earlier parts of this guide.

You may have a problem with "Can't create the configuration file" errors. If you do, set the wordpress directory to be owned by the www-data group:

sudo chown -R ubuntu:www-data wordpress/

from your home directory.

Ruby on Rails

Thusfar, we've used apt, a package manager, to get and install software. For a variety of reasons, the repositories that are used to pull in software using apt are sometimes a bit out of date - usually, this isn't a major problem, but in the case of Ruby and Rails, it tends to be.

Instead, we'll install Ruby using a tool called RVM, short for "ruby version manager". You can look up the current installation method at http://rvm.io. At the time of writing (and for the forseeable future) the command to run is

\curl -#L https://get.rvm.io | bash -s stable --autolibs=3 --ruby

Check https://rvm.io/rvm/install/ under "Install RVM with Ruby" for the most up-to-date command.

The RVM installation script will take a while to run. When it's done, it'll give you a message about running a "source" command in each of your terminals - you can do that, or just close all of your terminals, disconnect, and reconnect (note that if you're running tmux you must type "exit" in each terminal, then type "exit" after tmux exits, then reconnect!)

When you've reconnected, confirm that rvm is working by running the command "rvm". If there is a bunch of output, you're in good shape. If it says "function not found" or "not defined", try running the installation script again.

Now that rvm is installed, we'll install ruby (rather, a particular version of ruby). At the time of writing, the newest version of ruby is version 2.0.0, version p0, but it is very new - just a couple of weeks old. Instead, we'll install the tried-and-true 1.9.3-p392. So, run the command

rvm install 1.9.3-p392

If you get a message about "already installed", you're in good shape, if not, it should take a moment and install ruby for you. It is quite likely that by time you're reading this there is a more recent version of ruby - you should probably be using the most recent stable version as listed on http://www.ruby-lang.org/en/downloads/.

Now, we'll set that version of ruby as the default (feel free to replace this with a newer version if a newer version has been released):

rvm --default use 1.9.3-p392

(Note that that is a double dash before "default", not a single dash).

RVM comes with ruby gems already installed. So, we can go ahead and install rails. In order to make sure we have everything ready to go, go ahead and run the command *rvm requirements*

and find the line under the comment "For ruby:", which should look like

sudo apt-get --no-install-recommends install build-essential openssl libreadline6 libreadline6-dev curl git-core zlib1g zlib1g-dev libssl-dev libyaml-dev libsqlite3-dev sqlite3 libxml2-dev libxslt-dev autoconf libc6-dev libgdbm-dev ncurses-dev automake libtool bison subversion pkg-config libffi-dev

Run the command that is listed by rvm requirements (you should be able to copy and paste). Accept any confirmation questions by typing "y" and hitting enter. When complete, it's time to install rails:

gem install rails

It may take several minutes to install. If you get an error, try running

rvm reinstall 1.9.3-p392

and then re-running "gem install rails". Replace "1.9.3-p392" with the version you're using if you're installing a different version.

At this point, we are almost done. Let's make sure that everything is working by pulling up a test rails app. Go ahead and run

rails new testapp

to create a new application called "testapp", which we'll use to complete the installation. When the script is finished running, "cd" into the directory ("cd testapp"). Go ahead and look at the folders there by running "ls". (From now on, we're going to assume that you know how to change directories, find files using "ls", and edit files. If you get lost, reference the "Linux Crash Course" a few sections ago.)

If you want to run a development instance, just run the command "rails server" in the app folder. The application will be accessible on port 3000 - just append ":3000" to your server's URL or ip address, like "http://54.225.226.136:3000".

If you get an error that includes "Javascript Runtime Unavailable" (or can't determine the cause of the error), try installing node.js with

sudo apt-get install nodejs

To link Rails and nginx, we're going to use a gem called Passenger. So, we'll need to install it. This is easy to do, just run the command

gem install passenger

It may take some time to install. When it's done, we'll use passenger to install a new nginx module - run the command

rvmsudo passenger-install-nginx-module

(the "rvmsudo" runs "sudo" but with rvm, so we can access our ruby installation).The installer will ask you to edit several settings as you set it up. Press enter to start the installation. Passenger will probably tell you that you don't have all the software you need, "but don't worry, the installer will tell you how to install them" - go ahead and press enter if this occurs, and then copy and paste the command that it tells you to run (in bold) into a new terminal pane and run it. At the time of writing, this was

sudo apt-get install libcurl4-openssl-dev

(Passenger didn't include "sudo" in its instruction, but you should add it). When done, you can re-start the passenger installation by running the rvmsudo passenger-install-nginx-module command again.

This time, it won't tell you you need to install more software. It will give you two options, to let the installer download and install nginx for you, or to let you customize the nginx installation - go with option 1 by pressing 1.

It may take a moment to set up the installation before it asks you which directory you want to install to. The default, shown in a bracket, should be [/opt/nginx]. Go ahead and accept this by pressing enter.

The installer will now compile the passenger files, which may take some time and will produce a lot of output. Eventually, you should be greeted with a message that "Phusion Passenger was successfully installed!" and be told to press enter to continue. Do so.

Now you're done installing software. To tell nginx where it should be serving ruby files from, you need to edit the nignx configuration, which is located at /opt/nginx/conf/nginx.conf, assuming you accepted the default path for nginx during the installation. When you run the command to edit it, use "sudo" - your user doesn't own that file, so you need to invoke superuser privileges.

In the file, find the "server {" block. Go ahead and remove all the content between the opening { and the matching, closing }, several lines down. You'll have one server block per website you host. Make the server block read as follows:

server {

    listen 80;

    server_name localhost;

    root /home/ubuntu/testapp/public;

    passenger_enabled on;

}

If you put your test app in a folder other than the above listed "/home/ubuntu/testapp", change it as appropriate. However, you should ensure that the path points to the "public" subfolder.

We can install a script that will make starting and ending nginx a lot easier. Run the following commands, which will pull down an init script from Linode.

wget -O init-deb.sh http://library.linode.com/assets/660-init-deb.sh
sudo mv init-deb.sh /etc/init.d/nginx
sudo chmod +x /etc/init.d/nginx
sudo /usr/sbin/update-rc.d -f nginx defaults

At this point, the only thing to do is reload nginx to make it recognize passenger. Run the command *sudo service nginx restart*

Which will restart the nginx server. Your server is now live - test it by visting the IP address associated with your server in your browser.

When you have a domain name set up and have set up the name servers (see the previous sections) to point to your server's IP address, you can change the server block to replace "localhost" with your domain name. This will allow your server to host multiple websites - the correct instance of rails or php will be served according to the server_name parameter in nginx's configuration file.

Two notes: if you make any changes to nginx's configuration file, you need to run "sudo service nginx reload" to reload the configuration. If you make changes to your rails app and want to take them live, run "touch tmp/restart.txt" in your rails app folder.

There are a lot of things you can do to update and expand your configuration, but since you have a basic site up and running now, we've accomplished our mission.

Developing for Mobile

This is somewhat of a bonus section - we don't want to go into too much detail about mobile-specific issues. But we will provide some general guidance.

First, you've probably thought about making an app, but you probably don't need one. If you've already built a web app, what extra functionality could a native iOS or Android app provide? Although a native app could have better performance or higher reliability, chances are that your application isn't so complex so as to benefit greatly from those changes.

In addition, developing a native application is hard, and adds a lot of complexity to your application as a whole. Although it may be hard to believe, the sort of web programming that you've done in preparation for deploying for this guide is relatively forgiving and easy compared to building native applications, especially on mobile devices. This is not to say that you shouldn't build a native application if you have a compelling reason to, though: rather, we just want to caution you from starting work on an app before thinking hard about whether it is really worthwhile.

If you don't have an app, then you need a mobile website. Solution? Use a responsive design if you can (a responsive design is one html file with one css file that correctly displays on both small, mobile screens and full-sized laptop and desktop screens - there are plenty of templates out there, including WordPress themes). If you do, there isn't anything more to say about developing for mobile: just access your website from your mobile device, and it's done.

If you have to deploy a custom mobile site, then consider using a library like jQueryMobile (http://jquerymobile.com). Although it isn't the prettiest, it is pretty easy to use and has a lot of the look and feel of a native app.

Conclusions

Wordpress can seem daunting at first, but with just a little experimentation it can be incredibly powerful. If we were to give you any one suggestion for moving forward it would be to throw up a web page this afternoon and start tinkering. After taking a few hours to familiarize yourself with the layout, you'll start to find that you are able to make huge, sweeping changes to how your site looks and feels without much effort at all.

If you start looking at how different themes operate, you might even begin picking up a little bit of PHP as you see how certain tags affect each theme differently.

The important thing is not to be afraid to make mistakes, fixing them will almost never be harder than uploading a fresh copy of Wordpress.

Appendices

Other Development Platforms

The guide assumes that the reader is using windows because it is the most popular consumer operating system. However, you don't have to use windows for development - in fact, it's actually a lot easier to develop on OSX or Linux. Here are some tips for setting up development environments on those platforms. If you get stuck, a few google searches should help.

Setting up a development environment on OSX

OSX users can also use XAMPP for PHP and MySQL. Just click the "XAMPP for OSX" link and download the OSX version instead of the Windows version, then follow the installer prompts. Once XAMPP is installed, you can install WordPress in the same way - just replace windows folder routes with the appropriate ones for OSX.

Since neither of the authors of this document are OSX users, we don't want to lead you astray by providing resources that might not be useful. However, we're sure that with a few searches, you can figure out how to get stuff installed on OSX - it's a heck of a lot easier than on windows, to be sure.

Setting up a development environment in Linux

Linux users can also use XAMPP, or they can install the same software that we mention in the full guide on their native machine. Download the appropriate version of XAMPP from the XAMPP website.

For Rails, Linux users have it easy. The steps are basically the same - install ruby, install gem, install rails, run rails new, etc. Once the rails environment is set up, everything else is the same.

The only caveat for Linux users is that on Debian-based systems (including Ubuntu, Xubuntu, etc), the ruby and rails packages are not maintained well. Instead of using apt's packages, you should use a tool called rvm. Follow the instructions on rvm.io (which are also detailed in the "deploying a real server" section) to set up ruby - it will save significant hassle in the long run.

More Resources

If you need more help, there are thousands of resources around the net that can help you figure out whatever problem you're facing. The first step, as always, is a google search - that will probably take you to one of the resources we're listing here anyway.

- StackOverflow: http://stackoverflow.com is a great programmer-oriented question and answer site, the original website in the StackExchange network. It has millions of questions asked and answered for all sorts of programming related-topics - chances are, whatever problem you're facing has been faced by someone else on SO and answered there.
- ServerFault: http://serverfault.com is a sister to StackOverflow, but instead of focusing on programming and development, focuses on server administration. Worth

- checking out if you're having trouble with a running server or configuring a server program.
- IRC Channels: Although most internet users use instant messaging services like Facebook Messenger, Google Talk, or MSN messenger to stay in touch, the tech community still frequently uses IRC, or Internet Relay Chat. IRC has been around since the 90s, and is a pretty bare bones system, but more often than not there is an IRC channel somewhere with people willing to help you. You can google around for an IRC client that will meet your needs, and another search will let you find the channel you need to join for your problem. Note, though, that you shouldn't come into an IRC channel (chat room) without having exhausted your other options, first - nobody likes helping people who haven't tried to help themselves.
- RailsCasts: http://railscasts.com is a great resource for incredibly helpful how-to videos for different Rails-related topics. Most videos require a $9/mo subscription, but the free videos are still incredibly valuable.
- The Pragmatic Programmer: Actually a book publisher, however, anything published by them will probably be good.

Webhost Specific Tutorials

If you decide to go with the "easy" route a setup your web application using a VPS, you might find that each host does things a bit differently. Below is a list of brief tutorials on how to do everything from transfer files to properly setup a database for a number of popular web hosts.

Dreamhost

- Setting Up SFTP - http://wiki.dreamhost.com/SFTP
- Creating a MYSQL Database - http://wiki.dreamhost.com/MySQL#Creating_a_MySQL_Database_with_DreamHost
- Transferring Files - http://wiki.dreamhost.com/FTP
- Changing Name Servers - http://wiki.dreamhost.com/Configure_hosting_on_a_non-DreamHost_domain

Host Gator

- Setting Up SFTP - http://support.hostgator.com/articles/ftp/secure-ftp-sftp-and-ftps
- Creating a MYSQL Database - http://support.hostgator.com/articles/cpanel/how-do-i-create-a-mysql-database-a-user-and-then-delete-if-needed
- Transferring Files - http://www.hostgator.com/tutorials.shtml#ftp

- Changing Name Servers - http://www.hostgator.com/tutorials.shtml#other_registrars

Blue Host

- Setting Up SFTP - https://my.bluehost.com/cgi/help/248
- Creating a MYSQL Database - https://my.bluehost.com/cgi/help/6
- Transferring Files - https://my.bluehost.com/cgi/help/upload-site
- Changing Name Servers - https://my.bluehost.com/cgi/help/transfer_client_start

GoDaddy

- Creating a MYSQL Database - http://support.godaddy.com/help/article/36/creating-mysql-or-sql-server-databases-for-your-hosting-account
- Setting Up SFTP - http://support.godaddy.com/help/article/4942/enabling-ssh-on-your-linux-shared-hosting-account, http://support.godaddy.com/help/article/4943/using-ssh-to-connect-to-your-linux-shared-hosting-account?locale=en

- Transferring Files - http://support.godaddy.com/help/article/4598/how-to-ftp-to-your-server
- Changing Name Servers - http://support.godaddy.com/help/article/664/setting-nameservers-for-your-domain-names

About the Authors

James Gibson believes in numbers and code. He asserts that if something can't be quantified, then it doesn't exist – although he acknowledges that many things are rather hard to quantify. His friends correctly assume that, given the chance, he would probably turn himself into a robot.

Steve Spalding is a consultant, writer, thinker, Netflix watcher, Audible listener and all around Internet-type person who is a little bit obsessed with the idea of unlocking human potential and massaging these abilities into teams of super heroes charged with saving the world.

www.ingramcontent.com/pod-product-compliance
Lightning Source LLC
Chambersburg PA
CBHW070425180526
45158CB00017B/767